Love
FROM
Grandma

CHRISTOPHER SECULA

TO

GRANDMA TINA

FROM

8/31 ot   1st.

DATE   Bintadney

Happy Birthday

Love from Grandma

Revised and Edited

Copyright © 1995, 1998 Becky L. Amble

Published by Front Porch Books, a division of Garborg's, LLC
P.O. Box 20132
Bloomington, MN 55420

Design by Jennifer Parker

ISBN 1-58375-422-9

DEDICATION
To Grandma Betsey

ACKNOWLEDGMENTS
All the grandmothers

Norman Vincent Peale and Sybil Light of
the Peale Center for Christian Living

A special thank you to Tessie for her diligent help,
and to Dave and Louise for the hours of encouragement.

Thank you to all of the people who passed out my questionnaires,
and especially to all of the women who took the time to write
their advice. I wish we could have used everyone's material.

All of the grandmothers have given me permission to use
their first name, initial of their last name, age, and
either home town or current residence.

INTRODUCTION

I believe God made grandmothers different from everyone else. They seem to love unconditionally—just as God does—holding us close to their hearts, wanting to protect and guide us. If we will only take the time to look and listen, they are always there for us.

My own Grandma Betsey was a special person in my life—the only living grandparent I knew. My best memories are of sitting with her. We never had to do anything special—just be together.

The idea for this book developed out of my own workplace trend research as I noted high levels of stress and uncertainty among Americans at every age. After sending out over 200 questionnaires to grandmothers throughout America seeking messages they would like to share to help their grandchildren live a fulfilling life, this project took on a life of its own.

Love, From Grandma is more than a book of advice, it is a book of love. Maybe your grandmother is in this book, or maybe she is speaking through one of these grandmothers.

Becky L. Amble is an accomplished businesswoman, marketer, and researcher. She has been cited as a trend-spotter by The Wall Street Journal and USA Today. She works at the Minneapolis StarTribune as a group leader and marketing manager in the rentals market group. She is also involved with several professional, civic, and community groups.

Becky grew up in North Dakota and now lives with her husband, Marshall Gravdahl, their son, Alex, and two cats, AlleyCat and Greta, in Woodbury, Minnesota.

—— Foreword ——

Our grandmothers often define the very best in us. Childhood
memories of lessons learned at her knee become lessons to
be followed in adulthood. The grandmother's position is an
enviable one; all the good parts of listening and loving, playing
and reading, praising and spoiling without the daily routine and
problem solving. Her role allows nurturing and coaxing. From
the vaulted position of grandmother, she can speak volumes
about what's good and right and honest and pure.
A grandmother can instill values and morals and
truth through her wisdom and warmth.

NORMAN VINCENT PEALE

Pawling, New York

What is a Grandma?

The following was written by a third grader for a school assignment:

A grandma is a lady who has no children of her own, so she likes other people's little girls. Grandmas don't have anything to do except be here. They are so old they should not play hard. It is enough if they drive us to the supermarket where the pretend horse is and have lots of dimes ready, or if they take us for walks they should slow down past pretty things like leaves and caterpillars. Usually they are fat, but not too fat. They wear glasses and funny underwear. They can take their teeth and gums off. They don't have to be smart, only answer questions like why dogs hate cats and how come God isn't married. When they read to us they don't skip words or mind if it is the same story again. Everybody should try to have a grandma, especially if they don't have a television, because grandmas are the only grownups who have got time.

Thank you to Grandmother Patricia B.
of Palmer, Alaska for sending this to us.

Take care of yourself.
Love, Grandma

Life is a superb gift from God; treasure it!

Make the most of every day and every opportunity.

Each day is precious and filled with promise.

HARRIET B., 73, LAKE PARK, MINNESOTA

*Y*our future lies in your hands. Earn respect for who you are and what you stand for. Be strong about your beliefs and what you want to accomplish in life.

JANE W., 59, MINNEAPOLIS, MINNESOTA

*L*earn how to give and take in order to live as peacefully as you can. Peace within is the best happiness we can achieve.

LEONA H., 72, BILLINGS, MONTANA

*A*lways remember that you are unique;
there is no one else like you. You are a child of
a loving God and have inherent and infinite worth.
Understanding that enables you to fulfill your unique
potential, a condition for abundant living.

CHRISTINA S., 76, SPOKANE, WASHINGTON

*Life is like a play;
you have the leading role.
Make it an Oscar performance.*

KATHIE J., 50, LITTLE CANADA, MINNESOTA

A positive attitude will help you through difficult times and make life better for you and others. The way you live your life can make a difference; caring and kindness are contagious. God made you unique and special and He loves you no matter what.

EILEEN J., 62, RED WING, MINNESOTA

*O*nly you can determine what kind of life
you will lead, so make it meaningful. You have this
one life; fill it with all the joy and happiness you can.

HELEN B., 84, ROSEVILLE, MINNESOTA

*L*ove other people as brothers and sisters. Be kind,
courteous, and supportive. Meditate frequently on the Word
of God and look to Him for strength and guidance.

ROXANN M., 55, MOUNDS VIEW, MINNESOTA

$\mathcal{L}$ife is short and involves hard work,
so make it count for something. Remember
that no matter what you do, it always affects
someone else. Be ready not only to accept
congratulations, but also responsibility. Use
your mistakes as an opportunity to learn.

JEANETTE S., 57, MONTEREY, CALIFORNIA

$\mathcal{F}$ind your greatest contentment in your own company. Don't postpone the great adventure of reading biographies, history, short stories, and essays.

MARY G., 65, OMAHA, NEBRASKA

Be curious and
continue to
learn new things
as long as you
are able.

NELL S., 58, NEWMAN
GROVE, NEBRASKA

*J*ust be yourself; it's the way God made
you and it's very fulfilling. Learn self-control
and you will become a strong, genuinely
independent person. Don't act on impulse,
but think things through.

IRENE S., 57, ROTHSAY, MINNESOTA

$\mathcal{L}$ife is not always a bed of roses. Learn to accept

the disappointments or things you cannot change,

but stand tall and be proud of who you are.

WILMA H., 70, TULARE, SOUTH DAKOTA

$\mathcal{D}$o not pass up interesting opportunities. Learn from

experience. Do not be afraid to take chances. Life is a challenge;

roll with the punches, take a deep breath, and try again.

MARYONA J., 72, MILES CITY, MICHIGAN

$\mathscr{R}$emember that character, dignity, and

dependability are vital in life. Face your problems

squarely; don't leave them for another day or for

someone else to solve for you. Live each day as though

it were your last, because some opportunities

will not come your way again.

NORMA T., 85, RENO, NEVADA

*E*xperience your uniqueness. There is no one else on earth who has your combination of qualities. No one else on earth can make your observations or give your insights.

VIVIAN L., 73, MORA, MINNESOTA

Learn to laugh at your minor mistakes and to learn from the earth-shaking ones.

SHARON K., 50, CHICAGO, ILLINOIS

*L*ive your life as if everything you do will be on the front page of the newspaper. Have faith, and love your fellow man. Be determined and set examples for your own children. Show kindness to all.

LETA C., 70, MIDLAND, MICHIGAN

$\mathcal{T}$o "love your neighbor as yourself" starts by loving yourself and multiplies by sharing that love with others. Unconditional love brings a joyous energy that will surely bless your life with peace.

LOIS V., 54, CLEAR LAKE, WISCONSIN

$\mathcal{W}$hen you are tempted to follow the crowd, believe in yourself. Don't be afraid to be different. Everyone admires an individual who has principles.

DODIE P., 62, OTTAWA, CANADA

You will get out of life what you put into it. I have several "rules for life": Accentuate the positive. Do what comes naturally. Remember your roots. It's good to improve yourself, but never think that you are better than anyone else. Keep it simple.

The simple things in life are best!

KARLENE S., 59, HOLYOKE, MASSACHUSETTS

*R*eflect on your life. Reflect also on God. Knowledge of God is not passive. Read, listen, and reflect. Align yourself with others who do this.

BETTY M., 65, ROCHESTER, MINNESOTA

Everything you do, think, or say is very important. It does not matter what other people think. You know who you are and you are very special. God loves you and I love you.

PAT D., 57, MISSION, TEXAS

*S*et short-term goals first with long-term expectations. Don't be disappointed if you have to make adjustments. Life is full of adjustments and you have to learn to be flexible.

BONNIE P., 54, SEATTLE, WASHINGTON

Take care of your family
and friends.
Love, Grandma

Keep family ties strong. You need your independence, but a close family circle can help you through the tough times and give you great joy.

JUDY F., 59, WOLCOTT, INDIANA

*A*ctions really do speak louder than words. I believe that children are a reflection of their parents, and grandchildren are the blessings, the reward of a job well done. We all need someone to follow, someone to look up to; that's the privilege of being a grandmother.

GLORIA W., 69, FRANKLIN LAKES, NEW JERSEY

*F*amily and friends should be very
important to you in your everyday life.

JEAN K., 70, FORT DODGE, IOWA

*B*e grateful to your parents;
raising a child is not an easy task.

ALEXIA L., 64, CLEVELAND, OHIO

*"Riches" does not mean money alone.
Family, friendships, and health are
riches to be desired more than money.*

SHIRLEY R., 70, DAYTON, OHIO

When dating, always question whether you could be proud, happy, loving, and secure sharing life with that potential spouse. Looks and popularity are not the most important. Love, sincerity, and commitment are! Be selective, but realistic.

JAN A., 59, PRESCOTT, ARIZONA

Don't prepare so much for your wedding that you lose sight of the marriage.

BARBARA M., 65, MOUND, MINNESOTA

*C*hoose a lifetime partner whose family background, values, and goals are similar to yours. The same sort of church background is very helpful. If you differ, discuss your differences and their importance to you before marriage. Be prepared for disagreements and try to resolve them; don't run away at the first obstacle. Living together before marriage is not a commitment, but a "cop-out" which does not necessarily lead to a long, happy marriage.

MARTHA B., 72, CHARLOTTE, MICHIGAN

Bless your heart!

Take care of yo

Treasure

very proud of ye

God made you

grandchildren are a gift

*Y*our family loves you, so keep close to them
through letters, telephone calls, and visits.

LILLIAN J., 78, GRAND FORKS, NORTH DAKOTA

*A*lways try to communicate with your parents;
they are smarter than you think.

MARGE D., 58, REYNOLDS, INDIANA

*T*reat your parents with respect and don't forget to be proud of where you came from.

LaVonne H., 62, Moorhead, Minnesota

*S*ay "I love you" to those you do love.

Beatrice W., 62, Coon Rapids, Minnesota

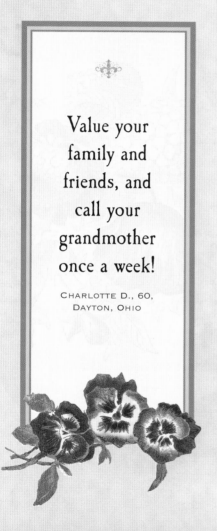

Value your
family and
friends, and
call your
grandmother
once a week!

CHARLOTTE D., 60,
DAYTON, OHIO

*L*et your children know you love them.
Spoil and enjoy them from infancy to
adulthood. But be firm with discipline and
explain why if necessary. Always praise their
efforts, no matter how minor. And keep
their imaginations alive. Children love
to hear stories of the old days.

ELIZABETH T., 70,
ST. CLAIR SHORES, MICHIGAN

Take care of others.
Love, Grandma

$\mathcal{B}$e loving and caring with people, for we are God's children.

Care for His creation and the gifts we have been given;

they are ours to borrow and pass on to others in better

condition than we found them in if possible.

CAROLYN C., 62, CRYSTAL, MINNESOTA

$\mathscr{E}$njoy all the gifts of life: nature, the arts,
literature, food. But most of all enjoy the people—
family, friends, community, and the chance
acquaintance. Listen, listen to what they say,
respect their thoughts, think upon them.

Jo G., 57, Red Lodge, Montana

$\mathcal{B}$e quick to say "I'm sorry" when you are to blame,
and mean it! Be slow to judge others, for as you judge,
so you will be judged. Be honest in all your dealings.

AGNES B., 85, SAN JOSE, CALIFORNIA

Don't always think about yourself.
What you give, in return will make
you feel much happier.

SHIRLEY P., 71, ROSEVILLE, MINNESOTA

$\mathcal{K}$eep in contact with friends and family; know that they are there to support you in any way that you need. Make new friends, too, to enrich and broaden your life.

CAROL P., 57, HARRISVILLE, RHODE ISLAND

$\mathcal{B}$e giving and forgiving. Seek out the good in people and love unconditionally. Be in control of your life, but don't try to control others.

PENNY B., 55, IRVING, TEXAS

*A*ccept, encourage, and support
how different we all are.

JUDY A., 57, BALDWIN, NEW YORK

*B*e loyal to your friends and keep a sense of humor. It helps
with life's downs. Don't let silly misunderstandings cause major
problems with friends or fellow workers. Be kind and try to see
both sides of a problem. Above all, my dear grandchild,
know that you are loved, and keep in touch.

DOROTHY G., 71, NORTHVILLE, MICHIGAN

*N*ever go against your good judgment to follow a peer or group in the wrong direction. Be strong, do right, and enjoy a successful life. Be considerate of others, especially the less fortunate.

THESTINA T., 84, GRAND FORKS, NORTH DAKOTA

*D*o not let unkind thoughts become unkind words.

PATRICIA B., 56, PALMER, ALASKA

*H*ave good manners always.
Be considerate of others. Try to
walk in someone else's shoes to
understand how he or she feels.

LaVonne H., 62, Moorhead, Minnesota

Be kind
to everyone,
especially
older people.

DOROTHY H., 83,
BEMIDJI, MINNESOTA

*L*ive your life with a positive attitude
and surround yourself with positive people.
Treat everyone you meet, young or old,
with kindness and an open mind.

EDITH G., 65, METHUEN, MASSACHUSETTS

*H*ave compassion instead of rebellion,

understanding instead of judgment,

and above all, have love and caring.

Always remember to respect people

for themselves and not for what

they can do for you.

ELIZABETH S., 71, KAMUELA, HAWAII

*M*anners are very important and will help you throughout your life. A smile and a friendly manner plus a genuine "thank you" can save the day!

IDA K., 70, ST. PAUL, MINNESOTA

*F*ill yourself with love, grace, warmth, and sensitivity. Do something for someone else every day of your life, preferably anonymously. Remember, God wants us to love others.

GRACIE G., 68, ALPENA, MICHIGAN

*T*hink before you speak. Saving a friendship is more important than saving face. Enjoy yourself, but never at someone else's expense. All people are God's children. We are in a diverse and interesting world.

DODIE P., 62, OTTAWA, ONTARIO, CANADA

Always be honest and open. Have good communication with others. Treat all people with respect regardless of race or income.

IRENE H., 70, AVON, MINNESOTA

$\mathcal{T}$o have a friend, you must be one. Friends of all ages make life interesting. Laugh and have fun. Do something to help others. There are so many good causes and so few volunteers.

LILLIAN J., 78, GRAND FORKS, NORTH DAKOTA

*G*et to know people of many races, religions, and cultures, and learn to appreciate their uniqueness. Share your ideas, dreams, time, talents, and material goods. Develop your ability to be a friend, to be caring and supportive. Above all, give God the glory in all good things that come your way.

MAE LOU T., 60, BERESFORD, SOUTH DAKOTA

$\mathcal{S}$how love, patience, and compassion. It is in giving, not getting, that our lives are blessed. Remember that a life worth living is filled with giving and forgiving.

RUTH R., 88, FORT DODGE, IOWA

$\mathcal{L}$earn from the mistakes and experiences of others as well as from your own.

MARY D., 54, PEORIA, ILLINOIS

*W*ork hard and apply yourself, but don't forget to enjoy life and your relationships. Try to see something positive in each and every person you come in contact with. Make friends with people from all walks of life and you will be a terrific adult.

DOROTHY B., 59, ST. PAUL, MINNESOTA

Regardless of how others treat you, think of how you would like to be treated and follow that path.

ETHEL S., 75,
WOODBURY, CONNECTICUT

*T*rust your instincts; trust your judgment. Never be cruel. Love all the creatures of the world. Love others. Love yourself.

LEE C., 75, MUNICH, GERMANY

Take care of your spirit.
Love, Grandma

Develop a strong spiritual life.
It will ease the problems and
difficulties of life and enhance
its joys and successes.

JO G., 57, RED LODGE, MONTANA

$\mathcal{T}$he best advice I can give is to have faith, hope, and charity. Have faith in God, a personal relationship with our living Savior, and faith in yourself. Have hope for the future and take a positive approach to everything. And have charity to share yourself and your talents with others and to give help to those who are in need.

OLIVE B., 62, HATTON, NORTH DAKOTA

*L*ive life each day fully for God. Greet each morning
with the prayer, "Lord, what are You and I going to do
together today? I'm reporting for duty."
You'll never be bored.

PEARL S., 62, HOUSTON, TEXAS

*P*rayer changes things. Trust in the Lord.

RUTH R., 88, FORT DODGE, IOWA

*When you were born you became a
gift to your family. You are a
special child of God.*

ELLA B., 62, TRONDHEIM, NORWAY

$\mathcal{L}$ove God, then love and care for yourself,

your family, and others—in this order.

If you truly love God and yourself,

everything else will fall into place.

KATHY P., 56, NEW MARKET, ALABAMA

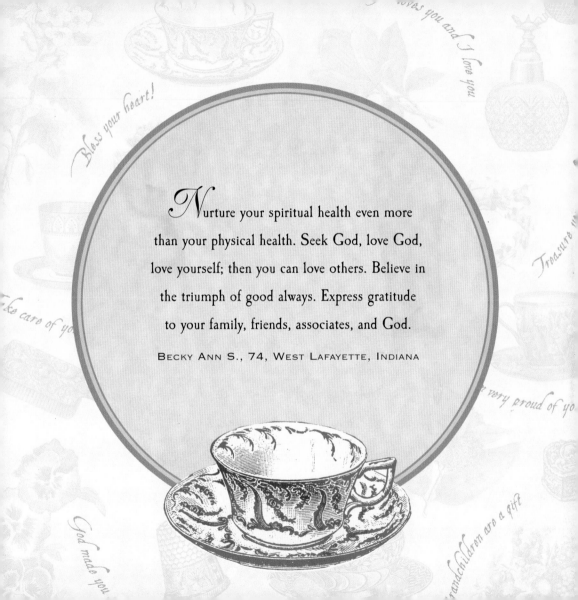

Nurture your spiritual health even more than your physical health. Seek God, love God, love yourself; then you can love others. Believe in the triumph of good always. Express gratitude to your family, friends, associates, and God.

BECKY ANN S., 74, WEST LAFAYETTE, INDIANA

If you start your day with prayer, God will lead

and guide you. Remember, God is on call

twenty-four hours a day.

ARLEEN K., 71, THOMPSON, NORTH DAKOTA

Always carry God's love with you. It will

enable you to understand and to forgive.

RUTH C., 77, SIOUX FALLS, SOUTH DAKOTA

*T*ake time to be quiet and talk to God. Enjoy the beauty of creation and preserve it. Above all, give God the glory in all good things that come your way.

MAE LOU T., 60, BERESFORD, SOUTH DAKOTA

You are a child
of a loving
God and have
inherent and
infinite worth.

CHRISTINA S., 76,
SPOKANE, WASHINGTON

*E*veryone you meet is made in
God's image. Give them the respect
and the dignity they deserve
as His children.

SANDY L., 47, PLYMOUTH, MINNESOTA

Stay close to the Lord; He'll give you guidance
and wisdom. You have to take time to receive it.
If you do there will be no challenge in your life
that His counsel cannot help you to solve.

HELEN B., 72, MINNEAPOLIS, MINNESOTA

*T*reasure honesty, both in listening to
the Spirit within and in dealing with all people.
Build a strong and personal relationship with God.
Do all you can to deepen that bond of love and
trust between the Creator and yourself.

MARIANNE W., 64, ST. PAUL, MINNESOTA

*A*lways take joy in the little things God gives you,

along with His greater gifts. Don't keep your

relationship with God too sacred. Talk to Him

when you're in the shower or stuck in traffic.

JUDY R., 48, BRECKENRIDGE, MINNESOTA

Become acquainted with God.
Talk to Him as you walk,
dream, or pray. He listens.

ALLEGRA V., 71, MIDLAND, MICHIGAN

Go to church and find friends there.

Try to find a good community to live in.

Start out, if possible, in a place where

you have friends and relatives.

MARION M., 75, CANBY, OREGON

*A*lways think of yourself as loved
by God, who is Love.

MARGARET MARY M., 70, MORRIS, MINNESOTA

*A*ttend Sunday School and church.
Believe in God. He will keep you on the right
path and help you through all your trials.

BEATRICE W., 62, COON RAPIDS, MINNESOTA

$\mathcal{L}$ife in all forms is a gift from God. If life
seems too complicated, return to your childhood
faith. You will see the right path to take.

MURIEL O., 68, THOMPSON, NORTH DAKOTA

$\mathcal{I}$f you make mistakes, ask God to forgive you
and accept that you are forgiven. Put a high value on
yourself. You are what God made you to be.

IRENE S., 57, ROTHSAY, MINNESOTA

*H*ave an abiding faith in our
loving God who created all things.
Choose Jesus, the way of love, and
you choose abundant, eternal life.

MARJ C., 74, ATWOOD, KANSAS

Say your prayers
every day.
Strong faith in
God can pull
you through the
darkest of times.

PATRICIA B., 56,
PALMER, ALASKA

*W*alk with God. Life is difficult and He has much to teach as you walk through, and grow because of, those hard times.

GERRY L., 57, GRAND FORKS, NORTH DAKOTA

*S*tay close to God, because with Him all things are possible. Keep prayer in your life and read inspirational material.

MARION D-H., 51, KNOXVILLE, TENNESSEE

Take care of your future. Love, Grandma

You have finally reached that point in your young life when you answer only to yourself. Sounds wonderful, doesn't it? Or does it feel a little scary? Remember, you have two of the most wonderful resources to turn to for encouragement, help, understanding, and most of all, love: your parents and God. When life gets tough, they will be there for you.

MARY ANN Z., 61, WOODBURY, MINNESOTA

$\mathcal{D}$on't expect the "good life" to be handed to you on a silver platter. Prepare yourself for life by getting a good education. Have goals and do your utmost to achieve them. Don't squander anything—your health, your resources, or the good old common sense you inherited. Don't take any of the above for granted. You can't buy them at any price. They are God's gift to you.

GLADYS S., 88, GRAND FORKS, NORTH DAKOTA

$\mathcal{T}$he world you live in is full of opportunities
to fulfill your every dream. You will be tempted in
many ways, but follow your good common sense
and don't be intimidated by anyone.

DOROTHY S., 72, MENOMONIE, WISCONSIN

*Decide what you really want to
do with your life, then set goals
so you can achieve it.*

BETTY S., 70, PONCA CITY, OKLAHOMA

Be honest and considerate; it will gain you
the trust of others. Without it you have nothing.
Money won't buy you happiness—only a few
material comforts. Friends, family, and time
for yourself should come before work.

SANDRA G., 52, PRINCETON, MINNESOTA

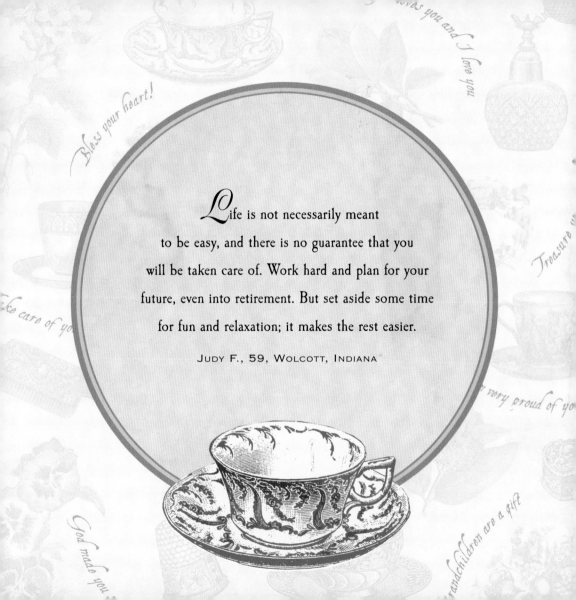

$\mathcal{L}$ife is not necessarily meant to be easy, and there is no guarantee that you will be taken care of. Work hard and plan for your future, even into retirement. But set aside some time for fun and relaxation; it makes the rest easier.

JUDY F., 59, WOLCOTT, INDIANA

*B*e cheerful and friendly to people. Have good
work ethics; show up for work and be on time.
Don't stand around and gossip, but try to keep busy.
Have good people skills and communication skills.
Obtain an education that will help you to support
yourself. Computer skills are important in this
day and age. Do not chew gum at work.

AGNES S., 84, CAVALIER, NORTH DAKOTA

*H*old on to your dreams. If you believe you can do it, you will. Set goals and take a step toward them each day.

MARION D-H., 51, KNOXVILLE, TENNESSEE

*Y*ou can't have everything overnight. Work diligently and you will begin to see the rewards.

S. JEANETTE F., 69, GRAND FORKS, NORTH DAKOTA

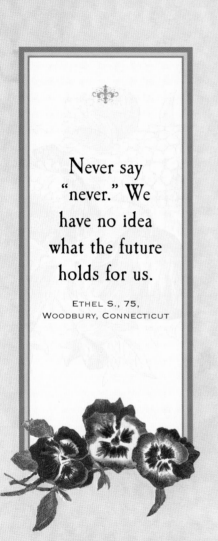

Never say
"never." We
have no idea
what the future
holds for us.

ETHEL S., 75,
WOODBURY, CONNECTICUT

*L*ife is the happiest and the most
worthwhile if you savor planting the seeds,
watching them grow, and nurturing them,
not just picking the fruit and the flowers.

BARBARA M., 65, MOUND, MINNESOTA

*W*hen we were children, we were so eager for life to move along quickly. Go slowly. Everything happens in its time. Life should not be fleeting. It should be slow, rich, and ideally, long.

KATHIE J., 50, LITTLE CANADA, MINNESOTA

*N*ever waver in your pursuits. Reach for the stars; many things are possible. The road of life brings many unexpected twists and turns. It is at these times that you must not swerve. Perhaps around the bend the road of life will again become straight.

FRANCES R., 89, HOLYOKE, MASSACHUSETTS

You are a very special person. Use your God-given talents, and remember that, no matter your age, your grandparents will be there for you.

LOIS W., 59, COLUMBUS, WISCONSIN

Be true to yourself and the principles you have been taught. You are a reflection of the people who have loved and raised you.

KARLEEN P., 57, HUDSON, WISCONSIN

$\mathcal{W}$hen you fall for any reason, pick yourself

up and start anew; after setbacks, you can go

forward to a better existence. Keep on

learning, which is the key to success.

PATRICIA N., 53, FRIDLEY, MINNESOTA

$\mathcal{B}$e happy when someone else wins the race,

the game, the money.

CATHY C., 54, MINNETONKA, MINNESOTA

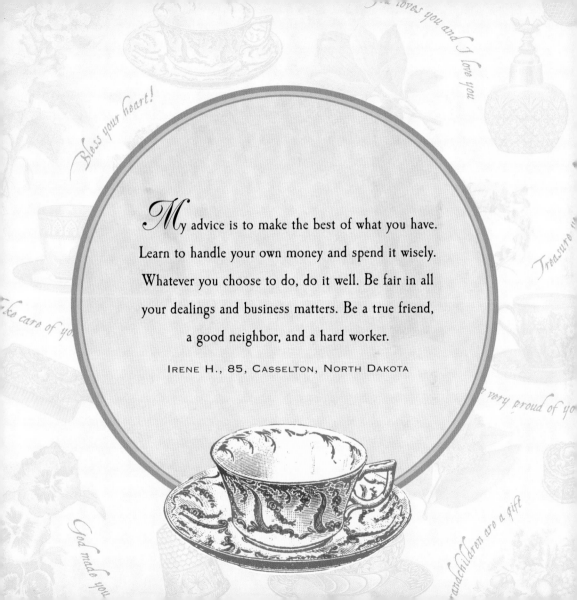

My advice is to make the best of what you have. Learn to handle your own money and spend it wisely. Whatever you choose to do, do it well. Be fair in all your dealings and business matters. Be a true friend, a good neighbor, and a hard worker.

IRENE H., 85, CASSELTON, NORTH DAKOTA

*Y*ou need short-term and long-term goals in your career, in your personal life, and in your spiritual life. Remember, your goals are yours alone, and only you can achieve them! If you miss your target, don't be discouraged. Bounce back! Re-evaluate, reorganize, and proceed!

JAN A., 59, PRESCOTT, ARIZONA

*K*now your craft and do it better than the others.

GERALDINE H., 79, KANSAS CITY, MISSOURI

*B*e clear about who you are and why
you are here. Have fun every day.
Learn from everything you do.
Ask plenty of questions.

BETSY B., 48, DULUTH, MINNESOTA

Develop a
positive attitude
and expect to
achieve success.
Your attitudes
are self-fulfilling.

GINGER J., 58,
PORTLAND, NORTH DAKOTA

Always save a percent of your income
regardless of how small the amount may be.
Tomorrow always comes; the sun keeps
rising and setting.

FLO E., 56, BISMARCK, NORTH DAKOTA

Take care of your values and beliefs.
Love, Grandma

Family and friends are all-important.
As you make choices today, consider how they
will affect you tomorrow. Be true to your values.

JEAN V., 71, BALDWIN, WISCONSIN

*V*alues are hard to keep in perspective, but to me they make our lives what they are. The words of advice that top my list are these:

Unselfishness. This is what "earns" love from family and gains you many friends. You can't live without them.

Honesty. When you are one of the oldies you'll not need to regret having hurt someone along the way.

Faith. This is the most important. There is Someone who cares very much about what happens to you.

MARGE B., 74, AUSTIN, MINNESOTA

*E*xamine and define your values. Do not choose to do anything that violates your values. Decisions will come more easily once this framework is in place.

MYRNA N., 56, PLANKINTON, SOUTH DAKOTA

Life is very short. Decide how you want to live it. Set your own direction and go for it!

MARY C., 57, HUDSON, WISCONSIN

*T*hough it is nice to be well thought of and respected, don't compromise your own values and ideas just to gain someone else's acceptance.

SHARON K., 50, CHICAGO, ILLINOIS

*P*lace spiritual values above everything.

ELEANOR B., 73, GOLDEN VALLEY, MINNESOTA

*L*et your conscience be your guide.
Don't allow a friend to talk you into doing
something you know is wrong.
You can say no! Be your own person.

BEATRICE W., 62, COON RAPIDS, MINNESOTA

*Y*ou can't go wrong with old-fashioned morality
based on the teachings of the Bible.

MARY JANE B., 75, CHICAGO, ILLINOIS

$\mathcal{G}$reet each day as a wonderful new challenge and a precious gift. You won't have time for preoccupation with past negatives.

PAT S., 71, LARGO, FLORIDA

*E*nduring values are better than
pleasure for the moment.

CAROLYN C., 62, CRYSTAL, MINNESOTA

*K*eep your word at any cost.

PRISCILLA G., 48, CAMARILLO, CALIFORNIA

As much as possible, live by the Golden Rule and the Ten Commandments.

JEWELL K., 82,
LYNNFIELD,
MASSACHUSETTS

Hold on to your convictions and don't be afraid to stand by them. Don't allow peer pressure to dictate your moves. Love yourself and like your actions.

PAT J., 59, LAKE VIEW, IOWA

Take care of all the rest.
Love, Grandma

———————

Share what you have and you will always be happy.

Happiness is not having what you want,

but wanting what you have.

MARIAN M., 70, ROSEVILLE, MINNESOTA

$\mathcal{M}$ake use of the abilities God has given you. Enjoy what is beautiful and believe that as you give to the world, so the world will give to you. Here is a saying that I like:

Do more than exist; live. Do more than touch; feel.
Do more than look; observe. Do more than read; absorb.
Do more than hear; listen. Do more than listen; understand.
Do more than think; ponder. Do more than talk; say something.

– John H. Rhoades

JANAHN E., 79, NEWMAN GROVE, NEBRASKA

$\mathcal{E}$xperience as many new adventures as you can.

KAROL W., 53, EVERETT, WASHINGTON

*D*o lots of reading. Cultivate a hobby or something to do when you're alone, such as reading. Nourish your spiritual life through books and prayer. Do something fun for exercise and eat healthy foods.

JEANNE C., 74, ST. PAUL, MINNESOTA

*L*earn to rejoice in the daily ordinary things and occurrences. Stay hope-filled.

MARIE G., 72, LAMBERTON, MINNESOTA

It's not what you have or how much you have, but who you have to share it with.

LORELIE A., 55, HASTINGS, MINNESOTA

*G*ive to the world the best you have and the best will come back to you. Practice honesty, unselfishness, fairness, compassion, integrity, self-discipline, and belief in God.

MARGARET F., 81, MELBOURNE, FLORIDA

*E*njoy life and get involved. Be conscious of and responsible for your actions. Stand up for your rights, but also know when to cooperate. Respect and consider the advice of others, especially your parents.

ANN K., 54, WALES, NORTH DAKOTA

$\mathcal{T}$ry to have a garden wherever you live, even if it's a pot on the front step. Plants are good for you and it's good to get your hands dirty now and then. Have fun. The kind of fun that makes you feel good. Clean fun, like a really good game of golf. Get a dog. You'll always have someone to come home to that really wants to see you. Find a friend, a real friend you can confide in. You won't need a psychiatrist. (The dog will help too.) When you look for the love of your life, don't look so much at the outside. Look with your heart, and when you marry, do so with the idea that you're doing this for life. Care about others. Laugh a lot.

JUDY R., 48, BRECKENRIDGE, MINNESOTA

I believe that life is an exciting adventure.
There are valleys and peaks and we must have a zest
for life, a positive attitude, and faith in God.

KAREN W., 48, DETROIT, MICHIGAN

*A*lways wear clean underwear in case
you're in an accident.

FLORENCE B., 82, RHINELANDER, WISCONSIN

*Y*ou will only have one lifetime.
Fill it full of good memories!

BETTY B., 79, SUN CITY, ARIZONA

Love ❀ _Grandma_

CHRISTOPHER:

No Matter where you are or how far
away I May Be I love you with All My
Heart and don't want you ever to forget
That. I'm so very proud of you as an
infant, and in my heart, know that, thru your
stages of Life you are going to Be Responsble
to love and Be loved for future Generations.
Make Good Choices! know Love and that Love
is God - Honest pure true sincere and
you will Always find & know Happiness
Don't ear forget Grandma Tina loves you
and no Matter where I Am - you are in my
Heart. Always. Follow your Heart to Be the
Man you want to be.
With Faith hope, sincerity Forgiveness and love
You will know God. From the day you were

Love 🌸 *Grandma*

Born, a grandma has cherished memories, and those memories are yours to hold on to thru your parents and Family

I will Always love you more Today than yesterd Because grandma's don't live Forever. But you will Be in our hearts for ever & ever and Ever — Always —

I Love you
Christopher Owen Secula

Love
Grandma TINA SECULA

Love 🌸 Grandma

Love 🌹 *Grandma*